MACHINES AT WORK

Tractors

Clive Gifford

 Crabtree Publishing Company

www.crabtreebooks.com

Crabtree Publishing Company
www.crabtreebooks.com
1-800-387-7650

616 Welland Ave.   PMB 59051, 350 FifthAve.
St.Catharines, ON.   59th Floor,
L2M 5V6   New York, NY 10118

Published by Crabtree Publishing in 2013

Author: Clive Gifford
Editorial director: Kathy Middleton
Editor: Wendy Scavuzzo
Designer: Elaine Wilkinson
Picture researcher: Clive Gifford
**Production coordinator and
    Prepress technician**: Ken Wright
Print coordinator: Katherine Berti

First published in 2012 by Wayland
(A division of Hachette Children's Books)
Copyright © Wayland 2012

Printed in Hong Kong/012013/BK20121102

Picture acknowledgements: The author and
publisher would like to thank the following
for allowing their pictures to be reproduced in
this publication: Cover (main) Shutterstock ©:
NanoStock; (inset) iStock © julia lidauer; pp2-3
Shutterstock ©: Elena Elisseeva; p4 Shutterstock
©: Rihardzz; p5(t) Shutterstock © Rihardzz,
(b) © Wayne Hutchinson/AgStock Images/
Corbis; p6 Shutterstock © Krivosheev Vitaly; p7
(t) Shutterstock © Luis Louro, (b) AFP/Getty
Images; p8 Shutterstock © Lucarelli Temistocle;
p9(t) © Tony Hertz/AgStock Images/Corbis, (b)
Shutterstock © Federico Rostagno; p10 Space
Factory / Shutterstock.com; p11(t) Stanislaw
Tokarski / Shutterstock.com, (b) Shutterstock ©
Graham Taylor; p12 iStock © Lya Cattel; p13(t)
Shutterstock ©DeshaCAM, (b) Shutterstock
©Leonid Ikan; p14. iStock © Steven Robertson;
p15(t) iStock © Cameron Pashak, (b);
Shutterstock ©Mikhail Malyshev; p16 (l) Rui
Manuel Teles Gomes / Shutterstock.com, (r)
© Paulo Fridman/Corbis; p17 Shutterstock ©
Palto; p18 Shutterstock © Stephen Mcsweeny;
p19(t) Shutterstock © JP Chretien, (b)
Shutterstock © Tish1; p20 Shutterstock © lculig
; p21 (t) ruzanna / Shutterstock.com, (b) AFP/
Getty Images; p22 Space Factory / Shutterstock.
com; p23 iStock © Cameron Pashak; p24
Shutterstock © Krivosheev Vitaly

**Library and Archives Canada
Cataloguing in Publication**
Gifford, Clive
        Tractors / Clive Gifford.
 (Machines at work)
Includes index.
Issued also in electronic formats.
ISBN 978-0-7787-1001-1 (bound).--ISBN 978-0-
7787-1005-9 (pbk.)
        1. Tractors--Juvenile literature. I. Title. II.
Series: Machines at work (St. Catharines, Ont.)

TL233.15.G53 2013   j629.225'2   C2012-907413-6

**Library of Congress
Cataloging-in-Publication Data**

CIP available at Library of Congress

Contents

Tractors at work

Tractors are vehicles with powerful **engines** and large, chunky tires. They can travel on roads at low speed, but they mostly operate in fields and on farms. All over the world, tens of thousands of tractors are busy at work.

FAST FACT

The first factory-made tractor, the Fordson, went on sale in the United States in 1917.

Engine is underneath body panels

Headlights allow the tractor to work in the dark.

A tractor drives through a field of hay. It tows a machine that turns the loose hay into bundles called **bales**.

ZOOM IN

The tall vertical tube on the outside of the tractor is called the exhaust pipe. When the engine burns **fuel,** the gases that are created leave the tractor through this pipe.

The **cab** is where the driver sits to operate the tractor.

Tractors are useful machines that can perform many different jobs. For example, on farms, tractors pull **plows** that break up the soil to make it ready for planting.

Large back wheels covered with rubber tires

This tractor is pulling a potato planting machine. The machine plants seed potatoes and covers them with a layer of soil. The seed potatoes will grow into potato plants.

Getting a grip

A tractor's engine burns fuel to provide the power that turns the wheels. As the wheels turn, the tractor travels forward. The force of **friction** helps the tires grip the ground.

FAST FACT

The TM1000 High Power is one of the world's largest tractor tires. With a height of 7.5 feet (2.3 m), this tire is taller than an adult man.

This tractor is a two-wheel-drive model. This means that only the two rear wheels are turned by the engine.

axle

Large rear wheels are joined together by a metal bar called an axle.

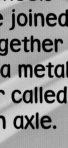

ZOOM IN

The pattern on a tire is called the **tread**. Tractor tires have a very chunky tread that helps them grip the ground well.

A tractor mostly works on rough ground or in muddy fields. Its large tires are filled with air. The tires are large so the weight of the tractor is spread over a larger area. This helps to prevent the tractor from sinking into the soil or mud.

This tractor works in paddy fields where rice is grown under water. Steel frames are attached to the rear wheels so the tractor can move easily in water and grip the ground well.

Driving a tractor

A tractor cab contains several controls. A foot pedal called an accelerator or throttle makes the tractor speed up. The **brake** pedal slows it down. Drivers use the steering wheel to turn the tractor to the left or right, or to make it go straight.

When the driver turns the steering wheel to the right, the front wheels of the tractor turn to the right.

FAST FACT

Most tractors rarely travel at speeds higher than 25 mph (40 km/h). The JCB Fastrac, however, has a top speed of more than 43.5 mph (70 km/h).

Many tractors can make tight turns. This is useful when a tractor has finished working on one row and has to turn sharply to drive back along the next row.

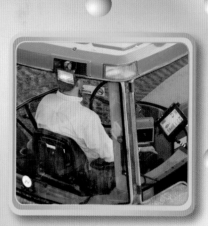

ZOOM IN

Some tractors are fitted with a special **navigation** system to help guide them in straight lines up and down a field.

This tractor is spraying rows of **crops** with chemicals to improve their growth. The driver has to steer carefully so the tires do not crush the plants.

Pulling power

A tractor is driven by a powerful engine. It generates enough force to move the tractor and any heavy farm machinery it may be towing, such as a trailer loaded with bales of hay. This makes a tractor a very useful vehicle to have on a farm.

FAST FACT

The Big Bud 747 is the world's largest farm tractor. It weighs 100,000 pounds (45,359 kg) when its 1,000 gallon (3,785 L) fuel tank is full.

This tractor in India is towing a trailer piled high with timber. Tractors tow many types of loads, including hay bales, fruits, vegetables, and fertilizer.

A tractor's pulling power is used to do a variety of work. Tractors can tow farm tools, pull unwanted tree stumps out of the ground, or haul out vehicles that are stuck in mud or water.

ZOOM IN

The tractor engine is covered by the hood. Tractor engines usually burn a type of fuel called diesel, which is made from oil.

This **crawler tractor** has tracks like a tank or bulldozer instead of wheels. These grip the sand well, allowing the tractor to tow a heavy lifeboat out of the sea.

Plowing and planting

Most tractors have a set of hitches at the back to allow different tools to be attached and towed. Some of these tools turn over the soil in a field and prepare it for planting seeds.

A plow turns over the broken-up soil.

A plow has large metal blades. These cut into the soil and break it up.

ZOOM IN

A tractor drags a tool called a harrow over a plowed field. The harrow has rows of long metal teeth or disks that break down large chunks of soil to make it ready for planting seeds.

When the field is ready, a tractor travels over it again, this time towing a seed drill. The seed drill makes grooves in the soil, then drops seeds into them. Once the seed is in the ground, the seed drill covers the seed with soil.

A tractor tows a seed drill to plant seeds that will grow into crops.

Hopper holds the seeds

Mowing and baling

Many tractors pull equipment that mow the tall hay in grassy fields and shape it into bales. The hay bales are stored in barns for farm animals to eat. The stalks left after harvesting cereal grains, such as wheat and rye, are also cut and baled. The dead stalks are called straw. Straw is used as bedding for animals.

This tractor is towing a hay mower. The mower's sharp blades turn to cut the hay. The hay is then left on the field to dry before it is baled.

Once the hay or straw is dry, tractors bring out the balers. These machines gather up the hay or straw, and pack and tie it into rectangular or round bales.

Baler opens at the back

Tied round bale of hay drops out

Inside this baler, rollers called drums roll the hay into a large round shape.

ZOOM IN

Bales can be rectangular or round. Their shape makes them easy for tractors to handle and to store in tall stacks.

Lifters and loaders

Some tractors are used around farms, forests, and other places to lift and carry different kinds of loads, from wood to soil to root vegetables such as turnips or carrots. To perform these tasks, special tools are attached to the tractor.

Many tractors are fitted with loaders. Loaders have a pair of long arms called booms attached to a large bucket. The bucket can scoop up many different materials, from rock and stone to crops or **manure**.

This tractor has been fitted with a lifting tool to pick up and carry large bales of hay. The tool can be moved up and down by a lever in the driver's cab.

ZOOM IN

Bale spikes on the end of a lifter or loader plunge into a hay bale. Friction between the spikes and hay makes the spikes grip the bale well for lifting and carrying.

A Brazilian farm worker pushes coffee beans into the bucket of a tractor loader. The tractor will carry the heavy load to the farm, where the beans will be put into bags.

Combine harvesters

When crops are fully grown, they are harvested. Cereal crops such as wheat and barley grow on long stalks. The stalks are cut and the useful grain is separated from the rest of the plant. This is all done by a machine called a combine harvester.

Grain tank can hold a large amount of grain

ZOOM IN

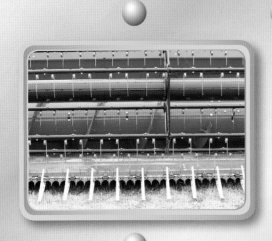

The reel at the front of the combine harvester is covered in metal spikes. The reel spins and pushes the grain stalks toward the cutter.

Inside the combine harvester, the grain is shaken off the stalks and stored in the large grain tank. The stalks are pushed out of the back of the harvester as straw.

Once all the grain has been separated, it is moved out of the tank through a long arm called an auger. The grain is pushed up the auger and falls into a big grain cart towed by a tractor. The tractor tows away the grain for storage in a grain bin.

Driver has clear view of field from the cab

Large front reel gathers in the stalks

A combine harvester can harvest a large field of wheat in less than an hour.

Tractors are such useful vehicles that they are found at work in many places other than farms. For example, smaller tractors are used in parks and on golf courses for digging, mowing and reseeding grass, and pulling out tree stumps.

This tractor is helping to clear snow away from a road. It has been fitted with a tool called an excavator bucket. This can scoop up snow and dump it away from the road.

Two tractors combine their pulling power to tow a large truck carrying hay bales out of a flooded area of land.

A tractor's pulling power can be used to tow many things besides farm tools. Tractors can pull smaller fishing boats out of the water and up a beach. Some tractors even take part in power pulling contests. The tractor that can pull a very heavy weight the furthest is the winner.

ZOOM IN

This tractor is pulling a carnival float at a festival in the city of Limassol in Cyprus. The float is carrying an entire orchestra!

Quiz

How much have you found out about tractors at work? Try this short quiz!

1. Which fuel is most commonly used to power tractor engines?
a) kerosene
b) diesel
c) paraffin

2. Which farm tool is used after a plow to break up chunks of soil and gets the ground ready for planting?
a) harrow
b) muckspreader
c) seed drill

3. What part of a combine harvester moves grain into a grain cart?
a) reel
b) auger
c) cab

4. When did the first factory-made tractor go on sale?
a) 1817
b) 1857
c) 1917

5. What device sticks into a block of hay to lift it up and carry it?
a) bale spike
b) bucker loader
c) hopper

6. What is the name of the largest farm tractor in the world?
a) Giant 920
b) Enormotrac 45000c
c) Big Bud 747

7. What part of a seed drill holds all the seeds?
a) drum
b) hopper
c) boom

8. What part of a combine harvester stores grain?
a) grain tank
b) grain boom
c) grain reel

Glossary

bales round or rectangular bundles of hay

brakes parts of a tractor that slow the vehicle's wheels down

cab the part of a tractor where the driver sits to operate the vehicle's controls

crawler tractor a tractor equipped with tracks or treads

crops plants grown in a farm's fields

engine the part of the tractor that generates power to turn the wheels

fertilizer a substance added to the soil to help it grow more crops

friction the force that slows movement between two objects that rub together

fuel gasoline, diesel, or another substance burned in an engine to create power to make the vehicle move

harvesting collecting a crop from farm fields

manure waste droppings from animals, often mixed with their straw bedding, which can be used in farm fields to make the soil richer

navigation system a device that helps a tractor drive accurately in the right direction

plow a farm tool that breaks up the soil to make it ready for planting

tread the pattern of grooves on the surface of a tire

Further information

Books

Tractors at Work, Lynn Peppas, Crabtree Publishing, 2011
Machines on the Move: Tractors, James Nixon, Franklin Watts, 2011
Vehicles on the Farm, Lynn Peppas, Crabtree Publishing, 2011

Websites

http://www.deere.com/wps/dcom/en_US/corporate/our_company/fans_visitors/kids/kids.page?
The kids section of the famous American tractor maker's website has games and videos showing tractors at work.

www.williamsbigbud.com/·
Learn lots more about the world's biggest farm tractor, the Big Bud 747, at this website.

www.youtractor.com/
A large, searchable, collection of videos of tractors and combine harvesters in action.

www.ntpapull.com
Learn more about the fun sport of tractor pulling at this website.

www.ytmag.com/gallery.htm
Yesterday's Tractors has photographs of hundreds of antique tractors of many different brands.

www.ext.colostate.edu/pubs/farmmgt/05016.html
General Tractor Safety page gives information about how to stay safe while operating a tractor.